Earth's Changing Climate

Natural Cycles and Climate Change

WORLD
BOOK

World Book
a Scott Fetzer company
Chicago

For information about other World Book publications, visit our website at www.worldbook.com or call 1-800-WORLDBK (967-5325).

For information about sales to schools and libraries, call 1-800-975-3250 (United States) or 1-800-837-5365 (Canada).

World Book, Inc.
180 North LaSalle Street
Suite 900
Chicago, Illinois 60601
USA

Library of Congress Cataloging-in-Publication Data

Title: Natural cycles and climate change.
Description: Chicago: World Book, a Scott Fetzer company, [2016] | Series: Earth's changing climate | Includes index.
Identifiers: LCCN 2015028050 | ISBN 9780716627111
Subjects: LCSH: Carbon cycle (Biogeochemistry)-- Juvenile literature. | Biogeochemical cycles--Juvenile literature. | Global environmental change--Juvenile literature. | Climatic changes--Juvenile literature.
Classification: LCC QH344 .N383 2015 | DDC 577.144--dc23
LC record available at http://lccn.loc.gov/2015028050

Earth's Changing Climate
ISBN: 978-0-7166-2705-0 (set, hc.)

Also available as:
ISBN: 978-0-7166-2721-0 (e-book, ePUB3)

Printed in China by Toppan Leefung Printing Ltd., Guangdong Province
2nd printing August 2016

Staff

Writer: Daniel Kenis

Executive Committee

President
Jim O'Rourke

Vice President and Editor in Chief
Paul A. Kobasa

Vice President, Finance
Donald D. Keller

Vice President, Marketing
Jean Lin

Director, Human Resources
Bev Ecker

Editorial

Director of Digital Product Content Development
Emily Kline

Manager, Science
Jeff De La Rosa

Editors, Science
Will Adams
Echo Gonzalez

Administrative Assistant
Annuals/Series Nonfiction
Ethel Matthews

Manager, Contracts & Compliance (Rights & Permissions)
Loranne K. Shields

Manager, Indexing Services
David Pofelski

Digital

Director of Digital Product Development
Erika Meller

Digital Product Manager
Lyndsie Manusos

Digital Product Coordinator
Matthew Werner

Manufacturing/ Production

Manufacturing Manager
Sandra Johnson

Production/Technology Manager
Anne Fritzinger

Proofreader
Nathalie Strassheim

Graphics and Design

Senior Art Director
Tom Evans

Senior Designers
Matt Carrington
Isaiah Sheppard
Don Di Sante

Senior Cartographer
John M. Rejba

Acknowledgments

Aurora Photos: 17 (Peter Essick). Getty Images: 43 (Diego Giudice, MCT). Landov: 41 (Nacho Doce, Reuters). Massachusetts Institute of Technology: 15 (Tanja Bosak). NASA: 5, 25. Science Source: 21 (Eye of Science). Shutterstock: 7 (Reluk), 9 (jopelka), 11 (Jason Benz Bennee), 13 (B. Brown), 23 (Deborah Benbrook), 27 (Dimedrol68), 29 (Jon Milnes), 31 (Ammit Jack), 33 (Platslee), 35 (Liushengfilm), 37 (Pan Demin), 39 (Nico Traut), 45 (Mimadeo). SuperStock: 19 (Matteo Chinellato, ChinellatoPhoto/Exactostock).

Table of contents

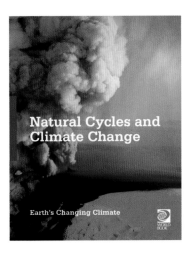

Natural Cycles and Climate Change

Earth's Changing Climate

A volcano in Iceland vents ash and volcanic gases. Volcanoes take long-buried carbon from Earth and return it to the atmosphere; this process is a part of the carbon cycle.

© Emil Thor Sigurdsson, Nordic Photos/Aurora Photos

Glossary There is a glossary of terms on page 46. Terms defined in the glossary are in type **that looks like this** on their first appearance on any spread (two facing pages).

Introduction

Earth is a world of **cycles.** Some cycles are familiar. Days bring warmth and light. Nights bring cooler temperatures and darkness. This cycle of sunrise and sunset repeats day after day.

Although each may feel a bit different, depending on where you are on the planet, there are seasons that come and go in a cycle. This cycle of seasons continues year after year.

Earth has more cycles than just days and seasons. Things that make up the planet constantly move and change. In Earth's **water cycle,** for example, water moves between the ocean, the sky, and land.

Ancient people knew about the water cycle. Other cycles have only recently been discovered by scientists. The *nutrients* (nourishing things) that plants use to grow move in cycles. And so does the chemical element carbon. (All elements are known by a symbol—a single letter or several letters. The symbol for carbon is C.) Small changes in the carbon cycle (see page 24) can cause large—and dangerous—changes in Earth's **climate.**

A photograph taken by an astronaut on the International Space Station shows clouds forming over Africa. Such clouds bring thunderstorms and heavy rains. These rains form part of the water cycle.

Elements

Everything on Earth—all *matter*—is made of **elements.** An element is like a building block of matter. These "element building blocks" can "stick" together, forming a **molecule.** Water, for example, is made up of molecules that are combinations of the elements oxygen (O) and hydrogen (H). Living things are made of more complex molecules that contain the element carbon (C). The elements carbon, oxygen, and nitrogen (N) form molecules that make up the air humans breathe.

Usually, elements on Earth are neither *created* (made) nor destroyed. However, molecules may break apart, and their elements may join up to form new molecules. These changes are called **chemical reactions.**

Elements move around the planet. They can travel from Earth's ocean, up into the sky, and then down to the ground. Elements can also move into and out of rocks. They can even travel into and out of the bodies of living things.

A **fungus,** such as this mushroom, breaks down the matter of living things that have died. The fungus then returns the elements to the ground so they can be used again.

The water cycle

The **water cycle** is the simplest natural **cycle.** In the water cycle, water changes form. Water can be a liquid, a solid (ice), or a gas (water vapor). When sunlight heats water, it *evaporates*—that is, it changes from liquid to gas, or vapor. Water vapor is invisible. But it forms a major part of the air.

In the sky, water vapor *condenses*—which means the water turns back into a liquid. Clouds are made of liquid water. The drops are so small that they hang in the sky. Eventually, the liquid water falls back to the oceans and the land as rain. If it is very cold, droplets of water in the sky freeze into ice. They fall as snow.

The water cycle brings water from the ocean up into the sky and down upon Earth's surface. Where water falls on the land, it forms rivers and lakes. It is also flows into the soil and collects underground.

Living things also are part of the water cycle. They cannot live without it. Plants *absorb* (take in) water. They also release water vapor into the air. Animals drink water and absorb water from plants they eat.

Global warming vs. climate change

The words *global warming* and *climate change* are often used to mean the same thing. These words are used to mean two very closely linked ideas. Global warming is the recent, *observed* (noticed) increase in **average global surface temperatures** on Earth. Climate change means the changes in **climate** linked to changes in average global temperature. Global average temperature has a complicated effect on climate. Global warming will not cause every place to get warmer. Instead, it will have a variety of effects on temperature, rain and snow, and other parts of climate. These effects are together called *climate change*.

Water vapor condenses into clouds.
Once condensed, some of the water falls
back to the ground in the form of rain.

The nitrogen cycle

Living things need more than water. The **element** nitrogen (N) is also necessary. **Molecules** that make up **proteins** contain nitrogen. Proteins provide *structure* (the form of things) and energy to all living things. The nitrogen **cycle** supplies living things with the nitrogen they need. In it, the element nitrogen moves through Earth's air, soil, and water, and into and out of its living things.

Nitrogen is normally a gas. It makes up about 78 percent of Earth's air. However, most living things cannot use the form of nitrogen found in the air. **Bacteria** are the key to the nitrogen cycle.

Bacteria are single-**celled** living things. (To compare, the human body is made up of trillions of cells. A trillion is a 1 with 12 zeroes behind it.) Certain kinds of bacteria that live in Earth's soil can take in nitrogen from the air. These bacteria change the nitrogen molecules into other kinds of nitrogen-containing molecules. Plants absorb these molecules from the soil. Animals get the nitrogen they need by eating plants.

When a plant or animal dies, bacteria can break down the body and return the nitrogen it held to the soil. This nitrogen can be taken up by other living things, like plants. Some of the nitrogen, however, can be changed by bacteria into nitrogen gas, completing the cycle.

Trees absorb nitrogen from the soil through their roots.

The phosphorus cycle

Phosphorus (P) is another **element** necessary for life. Plants and certain other living things use phosphorus (FOS fuhr uhs) in **photosynthesis** (FOH tuh SIHN thuh sihs). Photosynthesis is a way in which living things make food using the energy of sunlight. In animals, including humans, phosphorus forms an important part of bones and teeth. And all living things use phosphorus in special **molecules** that store energy.

Unlike nitrogen, phosphorus does not exist in the air. It is mostly locked away in the molecules of rocks. These rocks are called *phosphate rocks.* A process called *weathering* releases the phosphorus from phosphate rocks. In weathering, wind, rain, snow, and ice break down rocks gradually over many years. The phosphorus *seeps* (slowly goes) into the soil. Plants and other living things take it in. Animals eat these things, and phosphorus enters their bodies.

Phosphorus can also re-enter rocks from sediments. *Sediments* are bits of rocks, as well as shells and other *remains* (dead bodies) from once living things. Phosphorus-containing sediments wash into the ocean and sink. They become part of phosphate rocks at the bottom of the sea. Over millions of years, the motions of Earth's *crust* (outer layer) lift these phosphate rocks back onto land, and the **cycle** starts again.

A view of a phosphate mine photographed from above.

13

Why are these cycles important?

Earth is the only planet we know of with life. The **cycles** just explained do not just make life possible. Living things are part of these cycles and make the cycles possible. And through the cycles, living things have shaped Earth's nonliving **environment.** The nonliving parts of Earth also depend on these cycles.

To understand why the planet's life cycles are so important, it is helpful to think of the human body's cycles. A person's heartbeat cycles blood throughout the body. Breathing cycles air through the lungs. Without these cycles, blood, nutrients, and air could not spread through the body. The body would die.

Earth's cycles work in a similar way. They spread water, nitrogen, phosphorus, and other important chemicals around the world. Living things depend on these **elements** to live. But living things also work to pull these chemicals out of the environment. Without **bacteria,** for example, most nitrogen would never leave the air. Rainwater would wash nitrogen away without plants and the other living things that trap it in the soil.

Living things bring these chemicals together within **cells,** forming new molecules. These molecules spread around the environment as living things move around, eat, and die.

A bacteria making oxygen is shown in this photo. (The oxygen bubble is at the top of the bacteria, nearly ready to be released.)

Damaging the cycles

Humans have changed much of Earth's land. In changing the land, we have damaged the life **cycles** that we depend on.

One example of the damage caused by humans comes from *fertilizers* (things added to soil to make crops grow better) used in farming. Crops, like other plants, depend on nitrogen (N) and phosphorus (P) to grow. Fertilizer contains these two **elements.** To get better harvests, many farmers put fertilizer on their fields.

But the crops do not absorb all of the nitrogen and phosphorus. Rain washes any extra fertilizer into lakes, rivers, and bays.

Plantlike living things called **algae** live in such bodies of water. Like plants, algae also grow better with extra nitrogen and phosphorus. But the fertilizer makes them grow too fast. Eventually, the algae cover the water, blocking the sun. Algae need the sun to survive, like plants. So huge numbers of algae below the surface of the water die.

The dead algae, in turn, *decompose* (break down). Fish and other animals cannot live in water full of decomposing algae. So they die too—and decompose, in a harmful cycle. Damage caused by some ways of farming sometimes kills the living things in water.

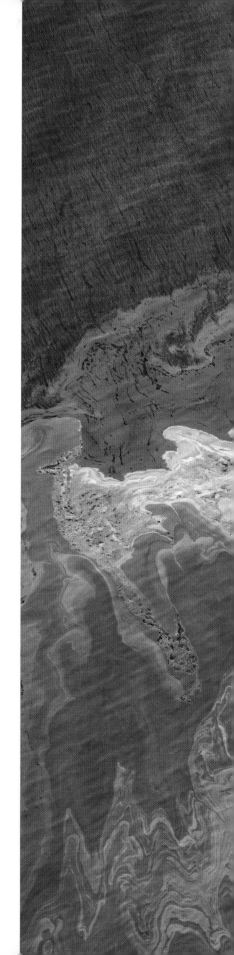

A mat of algae formed on Lake Erie in the summer of 2011. The mat was nearly 2,000 square miles (5,180 square kilometers) in size. That's the size of almost one million football fields.

What is carbon?

Carbon is the most basic **element** of life. In many ways, living things are built out of carbon. Life makes use of plenty of other elements. But carbon provides the structure, or form, of living things. It holds all the pieces of life together.

Carbon is special because of the shape of its **atoms.** An atom is a single unit of an element. **Molecules** are groups of atoms. Most atoms can link with only one or two other atoms. Carbon atoms are unusual, because they can link easily with four atoms at once.

Carbon's linking ability lets it combine in a huge number of ways. Carbon atoms can link up to form strong, stiff structures. Diamond, for example, is made of pure carbon. But carbon links can also form long, bendable chains. Plastics are made of carbon-containing molecules.

Living things contain extremely complicated molecules. Our **genes,** for example, are contained in a molecule called *DNA.* DNA is shaped like a long, twisting ladder. The "steps" of the ladder form the code—the hidden message—of life. They give the pattern for how living things should be put together. A DNA molecule is made of several types of elements. But without carbon, it would be impossible for these molecules to form. The other atoms would have no way to connect together in such a complicated shape.

Diamonds are made from carbon. Diamonds form in an area below Earth's *crust* (outer layer), under high temperatures and pressure.

Carbon dioxide

Carbon can be found outside of living things. It floats in the air—in the form of a gas called *carbon dioxide.* The **molecule** for carbon dioxide contains one carbon **atom** (C) and two oxygen atoms (O), so its symbol is CO_2.

Carbon dioxide has no color or smell. It forms less than one percent of the air. But even this little bit of carbon is important. Plants, **algae,** and certain other living things "breathe in" carbon dioxide. They depend on it to live and grow. In **photosynthesis,** plants combine carbon dioxide and water. They use these things and energy from sunlight to make their own food.

Animals, in turn, depend on plants and algae for their food. But animals do not breathe in carbon dioxide. They breathe it out. Plants take in the carbon dioxide that animals release. The breathing in and breathing out of carbon dioxide forms one part of the carbon **cycle.**

Wood, coal, oil, and gas—fossil fuels—contain carbon *compounds* (things made of more than one type of molecule). Burning these fuels also releases carbon dioxide into the air. This extra carbon dioxide can cause problems—because carbon dioxide has another important role. It helps control Earth's **climate.**

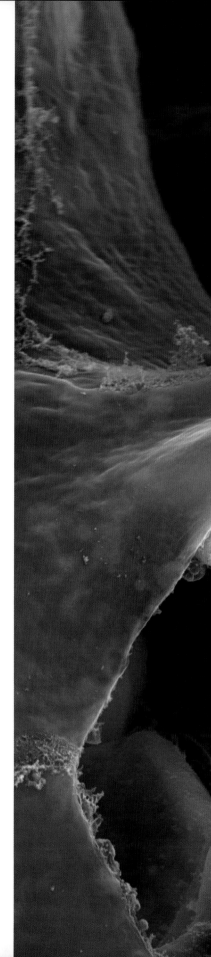

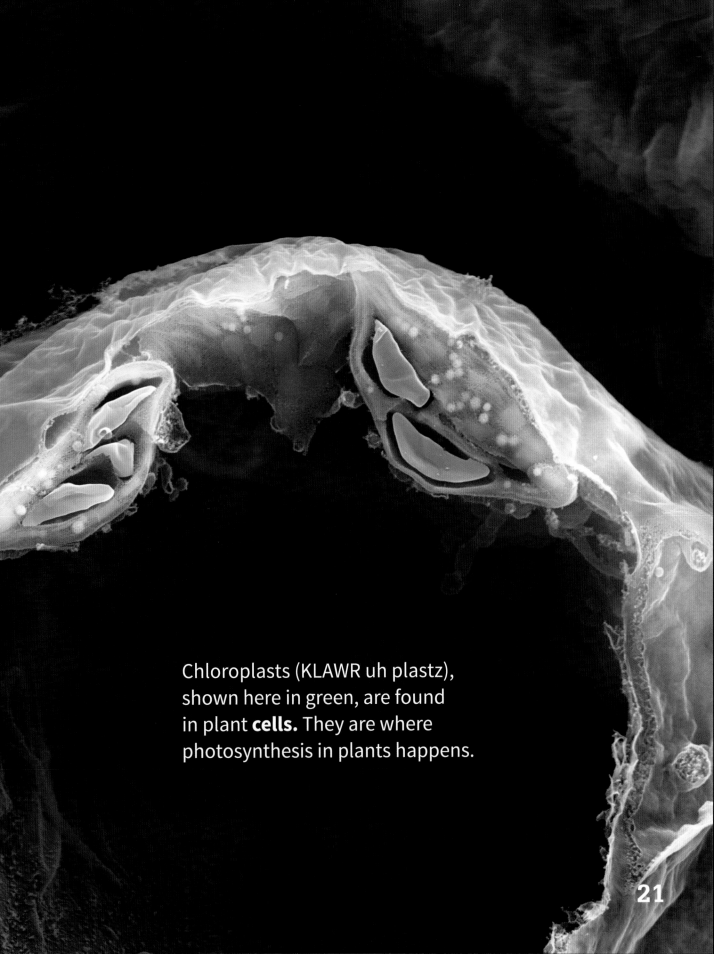

Chloroplasts (KLAWR uh plastz), shown here in green, are found in plant **cells.** They are where photosynthesis in plants happens.

Carbon dioxide and climate

Carbon dioxide makes up only a tiny amount of the **atmosphere.** But it is very important in Earth's **climate.** It acts like a blanket covering the world. If the blanket is too thin, Earth gets too cold. If it is too thick, Earth overheats.

Why is carbon dioxide so powerful? Unlike most other gases in the air, carbon dioxide is important to what scientists discovered and called the **greenhouse effect.** When sunlight strikes Earth's surface, some heat is *reflected* (thrown back) into the air. Most gases in the atmosphere let this heat pass straight through them. The heat goes out to space. Such a greenhouse gas as carbon dioxide, on the other hand, *absorbs* (takes in) the heat. It then releases it back toward Earth. The gas acts like the glass ceiling of a greenhouse. Small changes in the amount of greenhouse gases can lead to big changes in Earth's climate.

A power station can give off large amounts of carbon dioxide (CO_2). The tall chimney to the left in this photo is releasing CO_2. (The rest of the chimneys are cooling towers releasing water vapor.)

Other greenhouse gases

Carbon dioxide is not the only gas that causes the greenhouse effect. Water vapor in the air also traps heat on Earth. So does methane, a gas made of one carbon atom and four atoms of hydrogen (CH_4). But carbon dioxide is the **greenhouse gas** most closely related to human activities. That means we can control whether some of the carbon dioxide is released into the atmosphere.

The cycle of carbon

Not all of Earth's carbon is found in living things or carbon dioxide in the air. A lot of carbon is locked away in water and rocks. In fact, Earth contains about 3.5 quintillion (kwihn TIHL yuhn) tons (3.2 quintillion metric tons) of carbon. (The number for 1 quintillion is a 1 followed by 18 zeroes!)

Earth's total supply of carbon does not change. But **atoms** and **molecules** of carbon are constantly moving from place to place. This movement is the carbon **cycle.** Carbon moves through the air, the water, solid rocks, and the bodies of living things.

The carbon cycle is very complicated. It is also one of the most important of the life cycles. Living things are built out of carbon. And plants need to breathe in carbon (in the form of carbon dioxide) to live. Living things also depend on Earth's temperature staying steady. And carbon dioxide affects Earth's temperature. Each part of the carbon cycle affects the others.

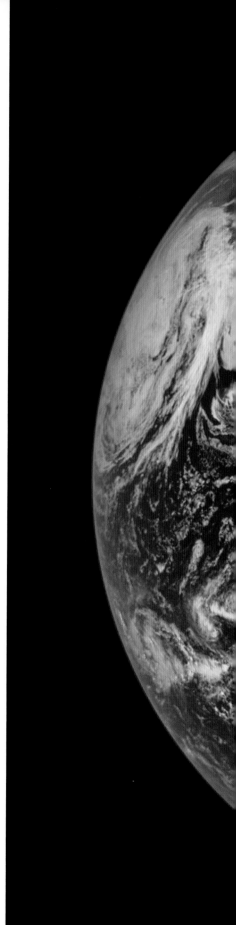

The weight of carbon

Carbon's weight of 3.5 quintillion tons on Earth seems like a lot. But carbon makes up only a tiny fraction of Earth's total *mass* (amount of matter)—less than one percent. Most of Earth's mass is made of the elements iron (Fe), oxygen (O), magnesium (Mg), and silicon (Si).

From air to life

Carbon is the building block of life. All living things use carbon. They *absorb* (take in), store it, and release it into the **environment.** But not all living things use carbon in the same way.

Producers are living things that take in carbon dioxide directly. Plants, for example, are producers. They absorb carbon dioxide from the air. They use this carbon dioxide in **photosynthesis,** which is how plants make their food. **Algae** are producers, too.

Consumers are living things that eat producers or that eat other consumers. Consumers cannot take in carbon dioxide directly. They get their energy from plants and other living things they eat. All animals are consumers, including humans. Consumers release carbon dioxide back into the air. Many animals, for example, breathe out carbon dioxide. (Fish release carbon dioxide through breathing parts called *gills.*)

In the carbon cycle, horses are consumers.
They take in carbon dioxide by eating
producers (the grasses).

27

From life to rocks

Most of Earth's carbon is locked away in rocks. Rocks do not "breathe in" carbon dioxide, as plants do. But rocks play a big role in removing carbon dioxide (CO_2) from the air. Carbon-containing rocks are called *carbonate rocks.*

CO_2 from the air *dissolves* into the ocean's water. (When a thing dissolves into a liquid, tiny bits of the thing spread throughout the liquid.) CO_2 can also combine with raindrops, forming a weak **acid.** This acid dissolves an **element** called calcium (Ca) in rocks. The rain carries the calcium into the ocean. There, it combines to form a **molecule** called calcium carbonate ($CaCO_3$).

Some $CaCO_3$ falls to the ocean floor. It makes up a rock called *limestone.* But most $CaCO_3$ comes from living things. Ocean creatures take calcium and carbonate from ocean water. They make calcium carbonate, which they use to create their shells.

Over time, shells, coral reefs (wall-like structures formed from the skeletons of small sea animals) and other structures become buried. *Sediment* (small pieces of rock and dirt that sink in water) covers them at the bottom of the ocean. The great weight of water and sediment squeezes these remains. They become limestone and other related rocks.

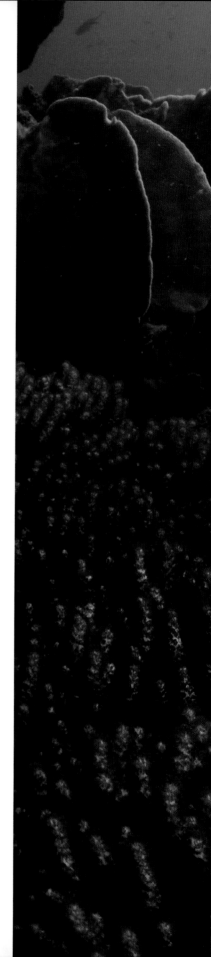

Some animals, such as the giant sea clam shown in this photograph, use calcium carbonate to make their shells. Over time, remains—shells and skeletons, for example—of such animals are buried and may become limestone, a carbonate rock.

From rocks to air

Limestone and other carbon-containing rocks lock away Earth's carbon deep beneath the oceans. How does this deep, buried carbon return to the air? Volcanoes.

Over millions of years, carbonate rocks get buried deeper and deeper. As more sediment piles up, the weight pressing down on these rocks becomes greater. The incredible pressure and heat beneath Earth eventually melts carbonate rocks.

The melting process causes **chemical reactions** (changes). One result of these reactions is that carbon dioxide separates from the melted rock material. But the carbon dioxide does not go anywhere. It is much like the bubbles of carbon dioxide in a can of soda. Earth's solid surface, like a soda can lid, prevents it from escaping into the air.

When a volcano *erupts* (throws out lava and ash), it is something like opening a can of bubbly soda. Magma—liquid rock—escapes from beneath Earth's surface. When the magma flows onto Earth's surface, it is called *lava.* At the same time, all the carbon dioxide escapes. Volcanoes can release huge amounts of carbon dioxide into Earth's **atmosphere.** Then, the **cycle** is complete—from air, to life, to rocks, and back to air.

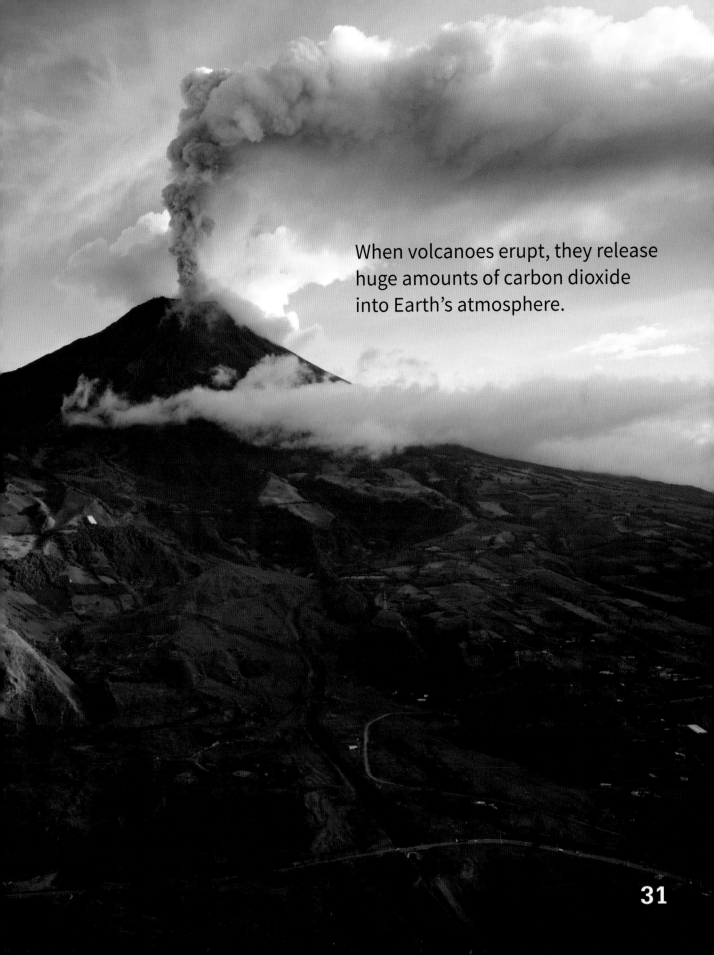

When volcanoes erupt, they release huge amounts of carbon dioxide into Earth's atmosphere.

How long does the carbon cycle take?

The carbon **cycle** is complicated. Carbon moves through the cycle at different speeds, depending on where in the cycle it is. Scientists sometimes divide the carbon cycle into two parts. The *fast carbon cycle* mostly involves living things. The *slow carbon cycle* mostly involves rocks and nonliving things. But, these two parts are tightly connected to each other.

In the fast carbon cycle, plants and other producers take in carbon dioxide from the air. As consumers (for example, animals) eat producers (plants), the carbon *cycles* (moves) through the food. Consumers breathe out carbon dioxide, completing the cycle. The fast carbon cycle is measured on a time scale of years. A **molecule** of carbon dioxide may only remain in the air for a few years before it is taken in by a plant.

In the slow carbon cycle, carbon moves between the air, the ocean, and rocks. It then joins the air again through volcanoes. This part of the cycle is far too slow to be affected by seasons. It takes millions of years for the slow carbon cycle to run its course.

Cliffs of limestone form a part of the slow carbon cycle. It may take millions of years for carbon locked in carbon-containing rock to move in the carbon cycle.

33

Fossil fuels

When living things die, the carbon in their *remains* (dead bodies) may become trapped underground. Mud may bury dead plants, **algae,** and other living things. Over millions of years, more mud and rock piles on top of these remains. Shells and other hard remains become limestone. The pressure from the weight of the mud and rock also squeezes other parts of the remains, changing them into coal, oil, or natural gas. These are called *fossil fuels.*

Fossil fuels are a very important energy source. Power plants burn coal or gas to generate electric power. Gasoline is made from oil and fuels most of our cars, buses, and trucks. People also use fossil fuels to heat their homes. Altogether, most of the energy people use today comes from fossil fuels.

In addition to energy, many important things we use come from fossil fuels. Plastics, for example, are made from oil. Fossil fuels are also used to make fertilizers and steel.

Fossil fuels are a *nonrenewable resource.* That means they cannot be regrown or replaced. Once we have used these fuels, they are gone. Today, our supply of fossil fuels is getting smaller.

Coal is a fossil fuel that is mined from the ground.

Uncovering fossil fuels

For most of human history, fossil fuels were rarely used. People have long burned small amounts of coal for heat. But most oil and natural gas lay too far beneath Earth's surface to reach. People did not know how to pump these fuels out of the ground.

Beginning about 250 years ago, however, the use of fossil fuel suddenly increased. The spark was the Industrial Revolution, a series of changes in manufacturing and society that began in Great Britain during the late 1700's. Steam engines powered British machines and factories. The burning of coal, in turn, powered the steam engines. As demand for manufactured goods increased, so did the use of coal.

And as machinery grew more powerful, so did the ability to dig deep into the ground. The *petroleum* (oil) industry began in the United States in the mid-1800's, with the first oil and gas wells. The invention of the automobile and gasoline engines further increased demand for oil. The fossil fuel became so valuable that people called it "black gold."

Soon, oil and gas wells were all around the world. And as people burned this fossil fuel, a lot of carbon dioxide rose into Earth's **atmosphere.**

Combustion

Combustion is the scientific word for *burning.* It is actually a **chemical reaction.** When heated, the carbon in fossil fuels reacts with the oxygen in the air. The result of this reaction: heat, light—in the form of fire—and carbon dioxide.

These machines, called *beam pumps,* bring oil up from deep in the ground.

Overloading the carbon cycle

Carbon dioxide doesn't stay in the air. Over time, the **molecules** get *absorbed* (taken in) by plants, or dissolved into the ocean, or formed into rock. Why, then, can't the carbon cycle just absorb all the carbon dioxide that comes from human activities?

The answer is that humans are releasing carbon too quickly. The huge increase in carbon dioxide has occurred just within the past few centuries. The fast carbon cycle can shuffle around this amount of carbon between living things and the air. But the amount of carbon still affects Earth's climate. It still works as a **greenhouse gas.**

The natural actions that bury the carbon deep beneath the ocean or lock it into rocks would truly remove its power to increase Earth's temperature. But this part of the cycle is much too slow to keep up with the amount of carbon our activities pump into the air.

Scientists believe that it would take hundreds of years for the carbon cycle to return to normal—and that's only if humans stopped burning all fossil fuels right away. These days, humans are burning more fossil fuels every year, and the amount of carbon dioxide continues to increase.

A tower is used to burn off extra gas at an oil plant. Burning off the extra gas prevents explosions, but it also adds carbon dioxide to the **atmosphere.**

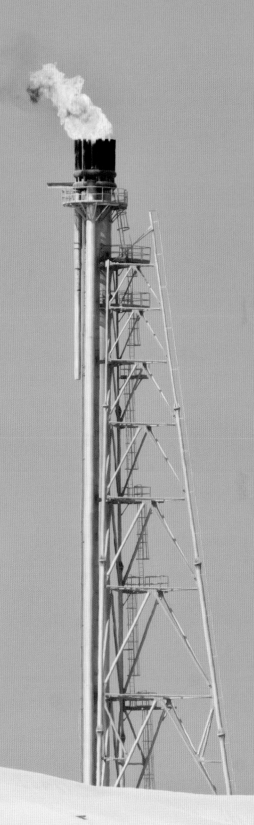

Carbon and forests

Trees and other plants *absorb* (take in) huge amounts of carbon dioxide. Because of this, large forests serve as important "sinks" for carbon dioxide.

However, there are not enough forests on Earth to absorb all the carbon going into the air now, year after year. And many forests are threatened by human activity. Such **rain forests** as the Amazon rain forest in South America are important carbon sinks. But *deforestation* (dee FAWR uh STAY shuhn)—cutting down such forests—is becoming a greater problem each year. With smaller forested areas, Earth can absorb less and less carbon dioxide.

A map of the Amazon rain forest

Every year, huge amounts of the Amazon rain forest are cut down by logging companies. The lighter green fields in the photo are farms where there was once rain forest.

The Amazon rain forest

The Amazon rain forest in South America is the largest rain forest in the world. But about 12 percent of the Amazon rain forest has been cut down or destroyed by people. And more of the forest is being lost all the time. Deforestation itself can add to higher amounts of carbon dioxide. Many forest areas used in farming are cleared by burning. The burning releases carbon dioxide from the plant material.

Carbon and crops

For thousands of years, humans have cleared forests to make room for farms. Modern *technology* (tools and ways to build goods) has sped up the process. Today, farms cover much of Earth's surface. Wheat, corn, rice, and other crops are plants that absorb carbon dioxide to live and grow. So why don't farms help prevent climate change?

The answer lies in the difference between crops and trees. A tree is a huge plant that absorbs a great deal of carbon dioxide. Forest soil also stores carbon. Plants that are used as food crops, on the other hand, are relatively small compared to trees. Because of that, they do not absorb as much carbon as trees. Their soil does not store as much carbon as does forest soil.

More important, crops are cut down and harvested every year. After the harvest, farmland does not absorb nearly as much carbon dioxide. In fact, the chopped stalks and other bits and pieces from the harvest actually release carbon dioxide into the air as they *decompose* (break down).

In addition, most farmers burn fossil fuels to harvest their crops. Tractors and *irrigation* (watering) systems require energy to run. This energy usually comes from burning fossil fuels.

Soil being prepared for planting on land that was once rain forest.

43

Vicious cycles

A *vicious (VIHSH uhs)* **cycle** is a harmful cycle that feeds on itself, becoming worse and worse. The carbon cycle's link to the **greenhouse effect** can create a vicious **climate** cycle. More carbon dioxide means a stronger greenhouse effect. A stronger greenhouse effect causes more ice to melt near Earth's north and south poles. Less ice means more open ocean, which absorbs more heat, which strengthens the greenhouse effect even more. Hotter temperatures could also cause deserts to spread. More deserts means fewer plants to absorb carbon, which leads to a stronger greenhouse effect—and so on.

If fixing the damaged cycles of nature is impossible—why even try? Because things could still get much worse. Pumping more carbon dioxide into the **atmosphere** won't just make it harder to restore the cycle to balance. It could lead to a disaster for Earth's climate and all living things.

Fortunately, people can still take action to prevent worse damage. Even individual choices, such as using less power in your home and recycling paper, glass, and metal can help shift the planet's cycles back into balance, bit by bit.

Wind turbines create power without using fossil fuels.

GLOSSARY and RESOURCES

acid A liquid that, when strong enough, is able to eat away solids and burn skin.

algae (singular, alga) Simple life forms that live in oceans, lakes, rivers, ponds, and moist soil. Some algae are tiny and are made up of just one cell, but others are large and contain many cells.

atmosphere The mass of gases that surrounds a planet.

atoms The building blocks of the simplest kinds of matter on Earth, the *chemical elements.* Familiar elements include hydrogen, oxygen, iron, and lead. Each element is made of one basic kind of atom. *Compounds* are more complex substances made of two or more kinds of atoms linked in units called *molecules.*

bacteria Simple living things made up of one cell.

cell The basic building unit of the bodies of living things. All living things are made up of one or more cells.

chemical reaction A chain of events by which one or more materials are converted into one or more different materials. For example, the chemicals carbon (C) and oxygen (O) can combine to form carbon dioxide (CO_2).

climate The weather of a place averaged over a period of time.

cycle The growth or actions that happen (in a special order) by which something undergoes a set of changes. Usually, cycles repeat themselves, the end circling around to a beginning—for example, with seasons, spring, summer, fall, winter, spring.

element Any substance that contains only one kind of atom. There are over 100 elements, each element is made up of atoms that are chemically alike.

environment Everything that is outside of a living thing, including temperature, food supply, and other living things.

fungus (plural fungi) Living things that get food by absorbing it (taking it in) from other living beings or from parts of such formerly living things as fallen trees.

gene The part of a cell that determines which traits living things inherit from their parents. For example, the shape of a plant's leaf or the eye color of a human being is controlled by genes.

greenhouse effect A warming of the lower atmosphere and surface of a planet by a process involving sunlight, gases, and atmospheric particles. On Earth, the greenhouse effect began long before humans existed. However, the amounts of heat-trapping atmospheric gases, called greenhouse gases, have increased a great deal since the mid-1800's, when modern industry became widespread.

molecule The smallest thing into which something can be divided and still have the chemical makeup of the original thing. Water is made up of the elements hydrogen and oxygen. A drop of water contains billions of water molecules. If one of those water molecules were separated from the rest, it would still be water. But if that water molecule were divided, only atoms of the elements hydrogen and oxygen would remain.

photosynthesis The chain of events in which green plant cells and other living things absorb (take in) sunlight and use the energy from the sunlight to make food. Plants need carbon dioxide and water for photosynthesis.

protein One of the materials that forms a necessary part of the cells of animals and plants. Proteins are made up mainly of the elements nitrogen, carbon, hydrogen, and oxygen.

rain forest A woodland of tall trees growing with year-round warmth and plentiful rainfall.

water cycle The never-ending movement of Earth's water. Water goes from the oceans to the air to the land and back to the oceans again.

Books:

Bang, Molly, and Penny Chisholm. *Buried Sunlight: How Fossil Fuels Have Changed the Earth.* New York: The Blue Sky Press, 2014.

Dakers, Diane. *The Carbon Cycle.* New York: Crabtree Pub., 2015.

Green, Dan, and Simon Basher. *Climate Change.* New York: Kingfisher, 2014.

Gardner, Robert. *Earth's Cycles: Green Science Projects about the Water Cycle, Photosynthesis, and More.* Berkeley Heights, NJ: Enslow, 2011.

Rothschild, David de. *Earth Matters.* New York: DK Pub., 2011.

Websites:

NASA – Changes in the Carbon Cycle
http://earthobservatory.nasa.gov/Features/CarbonCycle/page4.php

Science Education Resource Center – Climate and the Carbon Cycle
http://serc.carleton.edu/eslabs/carbon/

United States Environmental Protection Agency – A Student's Guide to Global Climate Change
http://www.epa.gov/climatestudents/

United States Environmental Protection Agency – Water Impacts of Climate Change
http://water.epa.gov/scitech/climatechange/Water-Impacts-of-Climate-Change.cf

Think about it:

From the seasons of Earth to the movement of the planets in our solar system, many things work in cycles. Can you think of things in nature that do not happen in cycles? For example, the eruption of a volcano does not really follow any regular cycle. Can you name more things without a cycle?

INDEX